RANGER RICK'S BEST FRIENDS

HI, I'M RANGER RICK, the official conservation symbol for young members of the National Wildlife Federation, and leader of the Ranger Rick Nature Clubs. On behalf of all the animals in Deep Green Wood, welcome to our world of nature and wildlife.

ELEPHANTS

by Robert Gray

**Created and Published by
The National Wildlife Federation
Washington, D.C.**

With tusk and trunk, this fellow can claim dinner any time. His super-long nose grabs branches. His super-long teeth dig roots.

4

ELEPHANTS ARE AMAZING

They're the LARGEST LAND MAMMALS ON EARTH. Some elephants weigh over twelve thousand pounds when full-grown, and stand eleven and a half feet tall. And those huge ears? Each is about the size of a standard bed.

40 Years

15 Years

6 Years

1 Year

Elephants are clever and easy to train. Each carries a trunk full of tricks . . . a nose that's trumpet, snorkel, pump, and also an arm and hand to gather food, heavy teak logs and lost baby elephants.

For delicate work, the African elephant has two finger-like tips at trunk's end. His smaller, rounder cousin from Asia has just one.

What would a grown bull like to eat in a day? Six hundred pounds of leafy branches and juicy fruit would do. And water? Forty gallons, if you please.

5

1 The Great Adventure

A bright, brass-colored sun blazed down from the cloudless sky. Mooli, an African elephant, rocked uncom- fortably from foot to foot. She was hot, dry, and miserable. The time had come to move her family to the shade

As the rainy season ends and clouds disappear, the parade begins:

6

of the forest at the edge of the plain.

Mooli's family was made up of twelve elephants. They were her sisters, cousins, children, grandchildren and even great grandchildren. Mooli, the largest and wisest elephant in the family, was their leader.

She led them away from the savanna (as the grasslands are called) at an easy pace. The big parade moved only three to five miles a day. Two kinds of birds rode along with the elephants. Tick birds pecked at insects burrowed in the folds of Mooli's hide. Egrets scooped up insects she raised with her feet.

with egrets on board, elephants leave the savanna to escape the hot sun.

7

The big elephants stopped often for food: for leaves and small branches of the savanna's acacias and baobabs; for fruit, bushes, and grass. They stopped to drink whenever they could.

At the water's edge, they met their savanna neighbors—zebras, giraffes, wildebeests and other antelopes. One day when Mooli stopped at a water hole, a large male elephant, a sire, joined them for the mating season.

Mooli was glad to see him and nuzzled up to him. Two years before he had also joined the herd. Now within Mooli was the calf he had sired. It would soon be born.

At last they arrived at the forest. It was a joyous time. The river was sweet and cool as it flowed among the thick growth. The sun's scorching rays were screened by the canopy of leafy branches. There was water to drink and plenty of food. For several days, Mooli lolled in the water and browsed on the trees.

Then one day Mooli asked two

At last... trees for shade and for eating;   water for drinking and bathing!

adult females called "Aunties" to join her. They went to a quiet, shaded spot among the trees, away from all the others. There Mooli dug up the earth with her front feet to make a soft and spongy bed for her new baby. While the Aunties stood by guarding her, Mooli gave birth to a male calf, whom she named Tembo.

Tembo weighed only two hundred pounds and was covered with a coat of soft, black hair. For several minnutes he lay on the soft cushion of earth. Mooli dusted him with dirt, much as a human mother powders her baby. She touched him with her trunk to learn his scent.

About twenty minutes after he was born, Tembo struggled to his feet for the first time. Mooli and the Aunties helped him with their trunks.

For a few moments he stood alone, wobbling and uncertain, confused by this big world he had entered so recently. He stumbled to his mother's side and instinctively nuzzled her body. Soon he was nursing, drinking her rich, warm milk.

Cows seek a secret place.

9

Loving young ones
help the baby
to his feet.

10

11

For the first few weeks after Tembo was born, Mooli watched over him constantly. When the sun became hot, she nudged him into the shade of her body. But as Tembo grew, he began to wander away from her side.

One day Mooli missed him. She searched the river. Tembo wasn't there. She looked in the underbrush. No Tembo! Then came his high-pitched squeal from beyond a small thicket. Mooli dashed among the trees toward the little one. She burst into a clearing . . . there stood Tembo, paralyzed with fear. A lioness was crouched in the short grass,

Using her trunk, mother gently prods her little one.

body low, tensed to attack.

Charging down on the surprised cat, Mooli's ears spread out like fierce wings. The big cat took one look at the angry elephant and ran.

When the lioness disappeared, Mooli turned to Tembo. He was all right, but frightened. With her trunk she spanked her naughty runaway; he should know that there were dangers in the world, animals to fear.

Then, the lesson having been taught, Mooli touched Tembo gently to make sure he was unharmed. And, using her trunk as a helping hand, Mooli led Tembo home.

Bath time! Come along now. There's room for us all.

2 Tembo's Test

Tembo stood apart from the others. They were all crowded together—his mother, his sisters and brothers, his cousins and aunts. They were his family. They were his friends. But they no longer wanted him. He was thirteen, the oldest of all the males. They had driven the other bachelors

out and now it was his time to leave.

Tembo walked slowly away. He glanced back at the herd sadly, then moved on. It was as if he had to go out into the world to face a test on his own, a test of his skill.

The sun was fiery. The ground was parched. The trees were bare. Rain, the desperately needed rain, had not yet begun to fall.

Tembo must search for food and shelter. He had done it many times, but always with other elephants. This time he must search alone. From others he had learned how to dig into the earth to find water. Now no one would help him.

There would be wild animals along the way—lions, dogs, and hyenas. But they would not bother him nor he them. Tembo wanted only grass, leaves, roots, and branches to eat. They wanted meat.

Tembo was sure that even the fiercest animal would not dare to attack him, for he was no longer a baby. He was over eleven feet tall and weighed more than five-thousand pounds.

So on he went, bravely and surely, across the dry plain, kicking up swirls of dust as he walked. He needed water. Where would he find it with no wise leader to show him the way? He needed food. Where should he look? He needed shade. It was nowhere in sight.

Tembo thought back to another

The family crowds around in distress. Earth is parched; bushes leafless and dry.

Big tusk pries, little trunk explores the juicy pith of the baobab tree.

year when the rains had come late, very late. Mooli had sheltered him in the shade of her body.

That was the first time he saw his mother push down a baobab tree that was beginning to lean. She dug her tusks into it to loosen the pulp and then started to gnaw on the good moist insides of the tree. Then she taught Tembo to do the same. But best of all she gave him milk even when the whole world seemed dry and comfortless. And she assured him that the rains would come again.

Baby's lucky. Mother still gives food and drink.

17

A water hole means a shower of joy.

blot out the sun. Thunder roared through the forest and across the plains. All at once big drops splattered down on Tembo's dry, cracked skin. Sand became streams and streams became rivers.

Then a new sound came, and Tembo spread wide his ears to listen. From out of the distance came a herd of gazelle. They bounded across his

Sure enough, one dry day the rains had come out of the thick, dark clouds. Tembo played that day with his brothers and sisters in the fast running water and the muddy pools that were filling up. Tembo could still remember how frightened he had been at first of the hard rain and then how happy. Now he wanted it to rain again in great showers.

Suddenly Tembo looked around him. Black clouds were beginning to

path, lightly drumming on the ground and bouncing like rain drops. The plains weren't empty. They were alive with life.

Small basins at Tembo's feet began to fill with water. Tembo sucked up a trunkful and pumped it into his mouth. He sucked up more and sprayed it over his body. Then he cried out in joy.

Someone answered. It was a young bull like himself. Tembo hurried to him. He would no longer be alone. They would travel together.

They raced to a broad hollow where the sloping sides had caught a bathful of rain. There they rolled and gamboled in the mud, the wet, wonderful, soothing mud.

Within days the grass and the trees

A king-sized pond gives two elephants a chance to frolic.

had turned green again. Soon other young bulls joined them. Now they were a herd of young bachelors.

The young bulls wandered in a group, stripping bark off trees and digging up tubers with their tusks. They reached high with their trunks for the choicest leaves and branches or pushed down trees to get at them.

They rollicked and played together and sometimes, for the sheer fun of it, they jousted. Then, it was forehead to forehead or ivory to ivory or trunk to trunk.

Tembo liked his new life, but something seemed to be missing. Then, one spring, Tembo watched a family of elephants making its way

Two stalwart tuskers stand face to face with trunks entwined,

slowly across the savanna. There were cows and their young. It was like the family Tembo grew up in, but Tembo didn't recognize any of them.

This was not Tembo's family, but he wanted to be with them and so he followed. When they stopped at a water hole, Tembo joined them.

None of the elephants objected.

Tembo was a full-grown bull now. He was strong and healthy and would sire the young of the family.

Tembo had met his first test. He had learned to live on his own amid the changing seasons of Africa. But now he would do even more. He would help bring forth a new generation of elephants.

ready to test their strengths above the river's muddy waters.

3 Working Partners

Lifting trunk tips above the river, two Asian elephants ferry men to the other side.

and pull the logs to market."

"Abdullah," said the Big Boss, "you will teach Kooma to carry the fodder for the other elephants. It will not be hard to do."

"Knock it down!" says the mahout.

In far-off India, Abdullah the Stable Boy raced to the stockade, his heart pounding. Here was Kooma the Wild, the new elephant the men had trapped. For three days they had pounded their way through the forest, driving Kooma before them. And now Kooma the Wild was captured.

"Abdullah," said the Big Boss, "Kooma will be yours. You will be his caretaker and trainer. You will be his mahout (ma-HOOT) forever."

"What job should I train him for?" Abdullah asked. "Will he ferry the men across the river? Or will he knock down the teak trees for us? Maybe he will lift the great logs with his tusks. Or if the logs are ready to be sold, he will wear the chain halter

◄ One elephant brings the food; another lifts the logs. ►

With hide painted and tusks bound, this Indian elephant is on display.

(Continued from page 25.)

Abdullah was disappointed. He wanted to teach Kooma something very special. But there would be time for that later. Now training begins.

First, Abdullah must win Kooma's confidence. The young mahout brought stalks of sugarcane for Kooma to eat. This was Kooma's favorite food. He walked Kooma between two trained females to teach him obedience. One day he climbed on Kooma's back. He spoke softly to the great animal and, gradually, Kooma began to understand the secret language shared only by mahouts and elephants.

Each evening, Abdullah took Kooma to the river to bathe and drink. Kooma would roll on his side in the cool water and let Abdullah scrub him with a coconut shell. After the bath, the young mahout swabbed him with oil to protect him from the hot Indian sun.

Slowly, Abdullah earned Kooma's trust. In return he gave Kooma the finest care. Soon they were partners, working partners for life.

Kooma proved himself a perfect elephant . . . peaceful, intelligent, and of even temper. And Abdullah proved himself a perfect mahout. It was then that Abdullah's great dream came true.

"Abdullah," said the Big Boss, "I want you to begin training Kooma to be a hunting elephant."

It was an honor; only the bravest and most even-mannered elephants can be good hunting animals.

Abdullah set dogs loose near Kooma to run and yap around his legs. He must not flinch. Abdullah tossed firecrackers in his path. He must not bolt. Kooma did well, and the great moment arrived.

"Now," said Abdullah, "you will carry the men who want to see the lions of Gir Forest and the tigers of India. We will go where there is danger on every side, but you will be Kooma the Brave."

Kooma was soon the favorite of all who came to India. But now Kooma is forty and retired. His tusks have been sawed off. Brass bands have been fastened around them. He is brightly painted and draped with beautiful cloths. Abdullah, now a grown man, parades Kooma through the city during religious festivals. Kooma is no longer Kooma the Wild, nor even Kooma the Brave. He is Kooma the Magnificent.

SAVING THE ELEPHANTS

A few thousand years ago, there were many different kinds of elephants roaming the earth throughout Africa, Asia, and even North America. Today all but two of these species are extinct.

What made them disappear everywhere but in Africa and Asia? Great changes in climate, perhaps. Experts do not know for sure. But they do know what danger the elephant faces today. Man is competing with the elephant for land and shooting those who invade his farms. And he has long hunted elephants for ivory.

In some African and Asian nations it is now illegal to shoot elephants or to trade in ivory. But men still hunt illegally and smuggle ivory.

Youngsters in African wildlife clubs are urging stricter enforcement of the laws and are also asking that more land be set aside for wildlife.

But how much land is enough for a herd of elephants? Some of Africa's young people want to help find out. To do this they will study Wildlife Management and then go out to the savanna to see if their ideas work. Let's hope these young scientists succeed, so there will still be elephants tomorrow.

BEFORE modern man arrived, forests offered elephants food and shelter.

AFTER man's coming, crops were planted; the elephant's home began to disappear.

With tusks that are worth gold in the world's markets, elephants need protection as they roam the open spaces of Asia and Africa.

29

WHERE ELEPHANTS LIVE

ELEPHANTS used to live nearly everywhere in **AFRICA**. Today they roam the central regions, with few in the far south and none in the north.

ELEPHANTS in quest of sugarcane roam freely in much of **INDIA** and **SOUTHEAST ASIA**, or labor industriously in forests and plantations under a mahout's care.

31

WHEN YOU SEE AN ELEPHANT

Take a close look at that incredible trunk. It is pleated like an accordion that can be stretched out or pulled up and curved around.

The tip is prehensile (pre-HEN-sil). It acts as a hand to grasp branches, or as fingers to pick up even the tiniest object.

Look at the legs, broad pillars to hold the elephant up. Look at the feet.

They have huge nails for digging up roots, and spongy cushions for padding silently and comfortably through forest and plain.

Would you like to know whether the elephant who is taking your peanut is from Africa or Asia? The African is taller and heavier than his Indian cousin. He has bigger ears and they drape over his shoulders and neck. His face is longer, his forehead flatter, his rump higher. But, poor fellow, he can't stretch out that marvelous trunk quite so far!

And now, if it is a hot day, take care. Your friend will want to spray himself with water to cool off and then powder himself with dust. So don't tease, or he may decide to spray you!

CREDITS

Dr. E. R. Degginger cover, African elephant herd; Leonard Lee Rue III pages 2-3, African bull elephant; 6-7, 14-15, 17, 32; Norman Myers, Bruce Coleman, Inc. 4, 18-19, 20-21; George Dineen, Photo Researchers, Inc. 8-9; His Royal Highness Prince Bernhard of the Netherlands 9; Simon Trevor 10-11, 16; Des Bartlett, Bruce Coleman, Inc. 12; Jen and Des Bartlett, Bruce Coleman, Inc. 13; Robert L. Fleming, Bruce Coleman, Inc. 22-23; Warren Garst, Tom Stack & Associates 24, 25 top; Jack Fields, Photo Researchers, Inc. 25 bottom; Stephanie Dinkins, Photo Researchers, Inc. 26; Robert Citron 28-29; Root/Okapia 29 top; Dale A. Zimmerman 29 bottom; Roger Tory Peterson back cover, baboon on rocks. Illustrations by Angeline Culfogienis 5, 27, 30-31; courtesy of Reader's Digest.

The Editors are grateful for text and picture assistance provided by the staffs of the Federation's Membership Publications—NATIONAL WILDIFE MAGAZINE, INTERNATIONAL WILDLIFE MAGAZINE, and RANGER RICK'S NATURE MAGAZINE.

NATIONAL WILDLIFE FEDERATION

Thomas L. Kimball	*Executive Vice President*
J. A. Brownridge	*Administrative Vice President*
James D. Davis	*Book Development*

Staff for This Book

EDITOR	Russell Bourne
ASSOCIATE EDITOR	Natalie S. Rifkin
ART DIRECTOR	Angeline Culfogienis
PRODUCTION AND PRINTING	Mel M. Baughman, Jr.
CONSULTANT	Dr. Henry Setzer
	The Smithsonian Institution

OUR OBJECTIVES

To encourage the intelligent management of the life-sustaining resources of the earth—its productive soil, its essential water sources, its protective forests and plantlife, and its dependent wildlife—and to promote and encourage the knowledge and appreciation of these resources, their interrelationship and wise use, without which there can be little hope for a continuing abundant life.